Contents

Getting started

Why business phrases?

As a business person, it is likely that you will sometimes need to use English in your work. A quick and easy route to learning English is to master key expressions that will be useful in a variety of business contexts. The business phrases featured in this book will help you communicate more effectively in a range of situations, including using the phone, sending everyday e-mails and taking part in the most common business activities in English such as company visits, meetings, giving presentations and making everyday arrangements.

What's in this book?

This book contains about one hundred and fifty business English phrases, chosen to reflect the modern business world in which mobile and electronic communications have a key role. The contexts are predominantly informal and reflect modern business practice.

It is divided into six chapters and a short section of idiomatic useful sayings. Certain phrases are highlighted on each page to draw your attention to key language. These key phrases are repeated in the **Business Phrases Index** at the back of the book. At the end of each chapter there is a **Review** section which tests your understanding. Answers to the exercises are in the **Answers** section at the back of the book.

Why is this book called a *Quick Guide*?

Because it guides you quickly to important phrases you need in business contexts and because you can learn these phrases in a short time. Spend ten minutes each day with this book and see how quickly you learn.

You can either work through the book from start to finish or choose a relevant chapter for a particular business need. Here is one way of working with the book.

- Choose a chapter that interests you. For example, *A business trip* presents useful phrases for meeting business contacts at their offices. Read the chapter. Try to memorise the phrases.

- Answer the questions in the **Review** at the end of the chapter. Then go to the **Answers** section. Were you right?

- Now go to the **Business Phrases Index**. Write the expressions in your own language.

A
business
trip

1

Directions to the office

A: **How do I get to your office?** Are you far from the town centre?

B: Not far.

A: Could you send me some directions?

B: **I'll send you a map.**

A: Is it easy to find?

B: Very easy, but **call me if you have any problems.**

I must have taken a wrong turning …

Arranging to meet a visitor (1)

A: **How are you planning to come tomorrow?** Are you going to drive?

B: No, I'll probably come by train.

A: **That's a good idea.** The station is only five minutes from the office. **Let me know what time your train arrives** and I'll meet you.

B: Oh, thanks. I look forward to seeing you.

I should have taken the train.

Arranging to meet a visitor (2)

A: **What time does your flight arrive?**

B: Five o'clock if it's on time. The flights are often delayed in the winter.

A: Well, good luck! **I'll wait for you in Arrivals. Call me when you're in the Baggage Hall.**

B: OK. See you later.

*My luggage
hasn't come
through yet.*

Arranging to meet a visitor (3)

A: **Can I pick you up from the hotel?** I could join you for breakfast or I could meet you in the lobby.

B: That's very kind of you but don't worry, **I can make my own way.** I'll either walk or take a taxi. **If I get lost, I'll phone you!**

I'd rather walk. I need some fresh air.

Security and reception

A: **Do I need a security pass to get in?**

B: Yes, you'll need one to get into the building. **Ask for me when you arrive at the security gate** and then leave your car in the visitor's car park. **I'll meet you at the reception desk.**

Later …

A: **I'm here to see Mr Stewart.**

C: Could you sign in, please?

Do you have an appointment?

19

Finding the office

To get to the accounts department, **take the lift to the fifth floor. Turn left out of the lift** and you'll see the door. Ring the buzzer and someone will let you in. **The marketing department is on the next floor up**, by the way.

OFFICE
PLAN

*I'm trying to
find the
logistics
department.*

Introductions (1)

A: **Have you met our human resources manager,** Joanna Fox?

B: No I haven't. Hello Joanna. My name's Dick Bird.

C: Hi.

A: **Joanna has been with us for five years. She's in charge of personnel matters.**

B: Pleased to meet you.

Do you know any of our production people?

Introductions (2)

A: **Let me introduce my colleague**, Ronan Erkum. Ronan has just joined the company.

B: **Good to meet you**, Ronan.

A: And you.

B: **How are you settling in?**

A: Fine. I'm really enjoying it.

How are you settling in?

Making conversation (1)

A: So what do you do, Dick?

B: **I'm responsible for staff development** at the Madrid office.

A: Do you work with Paloma Martinez?

B: Actually **I report to her**. She's my boss.

A: **Give her my regards when you next see her.**

B: I will.

I've been looking forward to meeting you.

Making conversation (2)

A: **How long are you going to be in Helsinki?**

B: Just a week. **I'd like to stay longer.**

A: **Is this your first visit?**

B: No, I come here quite often on business. It's a great city, especially in the springtime.

The new
consultant.

Welcoming

I'd like to welcome you to Inertia Manufacturing. Thank you all for coming.

I hope you had a good journey. First I'd like to give you some background information, and then run through this morning's programme.

… We'll come back here for coffee after we've been round the factory. **You can leave your belongings here.** I'll lock the room.

The factory tour should only take another two and a half hours.

Saying thank you

A: **Many thanks for your hospitality.** We're very pleased that you could come. **To show our appreciation, we'd like to present you with a small memento** of your visit.

B: **That's very kind of you.** I'll treasure it.

A: We hope to see you again soon.

That's very kind of you. I'll treasure it.

Problems

A: **I'm sorry, I don't remember your name.**

B: It's Tanya Nekrasov. We met in Moscow last year.

A: That's right. **Now I remember.** It was at the trade fair, wasn't it?

C: **Sorry I missed you earlier.**

D: That's OK. I managed to find my way to the office very easily.

Sorry, I can't find my keys.

More problems

A: **I'm afraid the conference room is reserved.**

B: Can't we use another room?

A: I'm sure we can find another room. **I'll just go and check.**

A: **Excuse me, I'm not feeling very well.**

B: Can I get you a glass of water?

Later …

A: That's better. Thanks.

I'm afraid the conference room is reserved.

Review 1

Key prepositions. Complete the sentences.

to (3)   *in*   *of* (2)   *with*   *for*

1 I'm responsible .... health and safety
   matters.
2 Who is in charge .... the Human Resources
   department?
3 Who do you report ....?
4 Have you been .... Tokyo before?
5 We would like to present you .... this small
   gift.
6 Take the stairs .... the third floor.
7 I'll meet you .... the hotel lobby.
8 It was kind .... you to send me a map.

Telephoning

Making a phone call

A: **Hello, is that John?**

B: Speaking.

A: Hi John. **It's about my trip to Warsaw next week.** I need to check some arrangements with you.

B: I'm pleased you called. **I was just about to ring you.**

I was just about to ring you.

Asking if someone is available

A: Is Mrs Safir there?

Possible responses

B: – Yes, **I'll get her for you.**

– **I'm afraid she isn't at her desk** at the moment.

– **She's on another line.**

– **She'll be back in the office next week.**

– Can I help you?

I'm afraid she isn't at her desk at the moment.

Transferring a caller

A: Can I speak to Luis Porto?

B: He isn't here at the moment. **Would you like to speak to his assistant?**

A: Yes, please.

Possible responses

B: – **Just a moment, I'll put you through.**

   – **Hold on please, I'll transfer you.**

WORLD CUP: TV. COVERAGE

FAX: IS ANY BODY THERE !?!

I'm afraid there's no answer on that extension.

45

Leaving messages

Hi John, it's Ulla. **I'm afraid I can't make the meeting** on Tuesday afternoon.

Could you call me back when you get this message? Speak to you later.

'Bye for now.

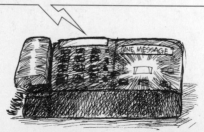

This is a message for Elinor Olvera. Hi Elinor. It's a quarter to eleven. **It's John Fox from Compass Securities returning your call. Can you ring me when you get this?** 'Bye.

Hi Val. **I thought it might be useful** for you to have a copy of the report I sent to Ulla, so I have posted it today. **Could you let me know when it arrives?** Speak to you later. Anton.

Hi Anton. **Just to say that I got your message** and I look forward to reading the report. 'Bye.

You have ten further options. If you have a query, press 1. If you require a brochure, press 2. If you need …

51

Calling back

A: **Thanks for calling earlier. I picked up your message.** Sorry I didn't call you sooner, but I haven't been able to contact Teresa yet.

B: That's OK. I understand.

A: **If I can get hold of her, I'll ring you back later this afternoon.**

B: OK. I'll speak to you then.

Sorry, I can't talk right now.

53

Phone problems

A: **Is this a good time to talk?**

B: Not really. Can I call you back? I'm in a meeting at the moment and I can't hear you very well.

A: Sorry, what did you say? **You're breaking up.**

B: I said I'll call you back. **Reception is very bad here.**

There's no
reception.
I can't get a
signal.

More phone problems

A: I tried to call you yesterday afternoon but **your switchboard was closed** and I didn't have your direct number.

B: Sorry, I didn't catch that. **It's a very bad line.**

A: Can you hear me? My battery's low so **we might get cut off.** I'll call you from another phone.

Review 2

A Complete the phrases.

dial   talk   leave   catch   say   cut   ring
get   hold   put

1 Sorry, did I .... you off?
2 Could you say that again. I didn't .... it.
3 Did you .... the message I left earlier?
4 Could you .... on? I'll see if she's in.
5 Would you like to .... a message?
6 First you need to .... 9 to get an outside line.
7 Could you .... me through to someone in Accounts.
8 I'll .... you back later this afternoon.
9 It's a very bad line. What did you ....?
10 I'm afraid I can't .... now. Let me call you back.

B Complete the questions with a–j.

1 When does ....?
2 What's the local time ....?
3 Can you transfer me ....?
4 Could you give me ....?
5 Does your battery need ....?
6 Could she call me back ....?
7 Do I need to dial 9 ....?
8 Are there any new messages ....?
9 Has everyone switched off ....?
10 Can I leave a message ....?

a) her mobile number
b) for someone in Customer Care
c) this afternoon
d) to the Sales office
e) charging
f) for me
g) their phones
h) to get an outside line
i) in Paris
j) your switchboard close

C Key prepositions. Complete the sentences.

for   *through*   *with*   *up*   *off* (2)   *on* (2)

1 I haven't been able to get in touch ....
  anyone in Sales.
2 Please turn your mobiles ..... We don't want
  any interruptions.
3 This is a message .... Pierre Flaubert.
4 I can't hear you very well. You're breaking
  .....
5 I'm afraid Sandra is .... another line. Can I
  help you?
6 I'll just put you .... hold.
7 I must have cut you .... when I dropped the
  phone.
8 I've been trying to get .... to the sales desk
  all morning!

E-mail
and the
Internet

3

E-mail addresses

A: **What's your e-mail address?**

B: **It's b p at b m e s dot co dot uk**
(bp@bmes.co.uk). I don't think I've got
yours.

A: It's tony underscore, rivers, all lower case,
at englishhomework, all one word, dot com
(tony_rivers@englishhomework.com). **I'll
be away next week but my mail will be
forwarded.**

Short e-mail messages

Hi John

Thanks for the message. I'm sorry to hear that you can't make Friday. **What about Tuesday morning? Let me know if that suits you** and I'll make the necessary arrangements. Could you also find out if Fiona can come?

Regards

Rona

Hi Ian

Just a quick message – I'm planning to send you the report as an attachment on Wednesday next week instead of Monday as there are some further details I need to check. **If I don't hear from you, I'll take it that this is OK.**

Best wishes

Rashid

Hi Pete

This is to let you know that we have just moved into our new offices and I thought you would like to have my new contact details. Our new address is ...

Ian

Thanks for sending me the details. By the way, I'll be out of the office until Tuesday next week but I'll be checking my e-mails. **If you need to get me on my mobile, the number is ...**

It will be difficult to contact me next week.

Surfing the net

A: Can you give me the web address again?

B: **It's English4 dot com, forward slash, business, hyphen, IT** (English4.com/business-IT).

A: Did you have a problem with the link back to the home page?

B: No, but **I couldn't download the information I needed**, the graphics wouldn't open and **there was something wrong with my printer.**

Did you virus-scan the file before you opened it?

Instructions

- **Click on the orange icon.**
- Right/Double click on the hyperlink.
- **Press the arrow key.**
- **Hold down the 'Alt' key.**
- Pull down the 'Tools' menu.
- Minimise/maximise the document.
- **Don't forget to back up your work.**

Whatever you do, don't press 'delete' or you'll lose everything.

Where is it?

A: I can't find it.

Possible responses

B: **It's in the top left hand corner of the screen.**

It should be under 'Tools'.

It's just above the 'Edit' button.

It's at the bottom of the screen.

It's right in the middle of the screen.

73

Computer problems

A: What's the problem?

B: We've got problems with the network. **Our server is down at the moment** and **my computer screen keeps freezing.** I can't get into the system.

A: Don't worry. Send me a message to let me know when everything is back to normal.

B: Now **my computer has crashed.** It's a disaster.

Is that the Helpdesk? I think I might have a slight problem.

More computer problems

A: Every time I try to open an attachment, **I keep getting an error message.** Any idea what the problem might be?

B: **What version of the software are you using?**

A: It's 2.4. It's quite out of date now.

A: That must be the problem. **You need to load a later version.** In the meantime I'll send the attachment in a different format.

It's about time we put in a new computer system.

Review 3

A Complete the phrases.

*menu wrong corner format attachment
date scan key*

1 The information on the company website is out of ..... .
2 I'm sorry – I forgot to include the ..... .
3 Could you send the file in a different ....?
4 I need to update my virus-.... software.
5 You need to look in the 'Properties' ..... .
6 There's something .... with my PC. It keeps crashing.
7 Look in the bottom right-hand .... of the screen.
8 Did you press the 'delete' ....?

B Complete the message. Put the phrases in order.

This is to let you know that unfortunately …

a) I'll see you at the hotel at 2 pm.
b) If I don't hear from you, I'll take it that this is OK.
c) What about meeting the week after next instead?
d) I won't be able to meet you in Amsterdam next week as planned.
e) Look forward to seeing then.
f) I can make the Wednesday afternoon if that suits you.

1☐ 2☐ 3☐ 4☐ 5☐ 6☐

C Key prepositions. Complete the sentences.

from in up at (2) *out to*
on with under

1 The e-mail address is info@(....)
   pearson-ema.com.
2 You need to click .... the hyperlink.
3 Are you sure the printer is plugged ....?
4 It's just .... the tool bar.
5 Don't forget to back .... your work.
6 The button you need is right .... the top of
   the screen.
7 Did you find .... how to open the
   attachment?
8 The link back .... the home page didn't
   work.
9 We're having a lot of problems .... our
   printers.
10 If I don't hear .... you, I'll go ahead.

Presenting

4

Beginnings

Good morning, everyone. **I'd like to tell you something about what we do here. First of all, I'll give you an overview of the company.** If we have time, I'd like to outline our development plans. **Please feel free to ask questions.**

*Could I
have your
attention,
please?*

Graphs

Have a look at this graph. It shows the total sales to date.

The year is shown on the horizontal axis and sales volume on vertical axis.

The dotted line indicates sales in the same period last year.

Sales fell in the first quarter of the year. They were at their lowest point in March; they peaked in October; there was a stable period between May and July; **the overall trend is upwards**.

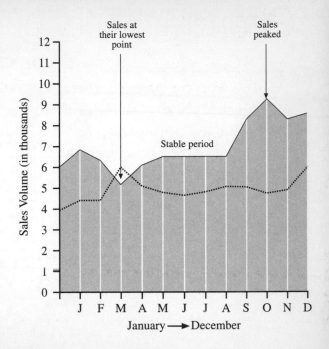

Charts

A: **This chart compares sales by geographical area.** The hatched section represents sales to the Middle East. If you **compare the chart with the one I showed you earlier**, you will notice a number of similarities.

B: **What percentage of sales goes to Argentina?** What about sales to Japan?

This chart shows a breakdown of sales by geographical area.

Middle East
Europe
Asia
Africa
USA
Latin America

SALES

Tables

Here are some other statistics. As you can see from the table, there are going to be big changes in the company. **The figures demonstrate** how the company will change over the next three years. We will become far more customer-focussed.

Phrases to describe rises and falls

- The number of people employed has declined in recent years
- Numbers have fallen
- Numbers have risen

As you can see from the figures, far more staff will soon be in service and sales.

STAFF	Year 1	Year 2	Year 3
Administration	20%	20%	15%
Production	55%	50%	40%
Service & Sales	25%	30%	45%

Moving on

Some phrases to keep the presentation flowing

- **Let's move on to the next slide.**
- That brings me to my next point.
- **I'd like to come back to that later.**
- Now something about …
- I'd now like to turn to the question of …
- **Could you turn to page 9** of the document in front of you …?

Let's have a quick look at the figures for next year.

Asking questions

A: I have a question ... **Can I ask a question?**

B: Yes, of course.

A: If I could make one comment.

B: **Go ahead.**

A: **I'd like to go back to something you said earlier.**

*I have just
one more
question …*

Clarification

A: **Can you explain what 'biztecno' means?**

B: I'm sorry, I have no idea.

A: **Is it something to do with technology?**

A: **What does BMES stand for?**

B: It stands for 'Business and Medical English Services.'

A: Is that a language training organisation?

B: I think so.

What do you mean by 'We need to let some people go'?

Endings

That's all I wanted to say for now. Does anyone have any questions?

... **Is there anything else you would like to cover?**

... OK, **I hope that this session has been informative** and I look forward to seeing you in two weeks' time.

I'd now like to hand over to our marketing manager.

97

Problems

A: **I'm sorry, but I can't see the screen very well.**

B: Is that better?

A: Much better, thanks.

A: I'm sorry, but I don't have the information with me.

B: **If you give me your address, I'll send it to you.**

A: How does this machine work?

B: **First we need to check if it's plugged in.**

Review 4

Key prepositions. Complete the sentences.

of (2) *for* (2) *from* *at* *by*
on *about* *in*

1 I'd like to talk .... what we do here.
2 This is a brief overview .... the company.
3 Can we move .... to the next point?
4 The graph shows sales .... the first quarter.
5 Numbers have fallen, as you can see .... the
   table.
6 I have a question .... you.
7 Does the I in IBE stand .... International?
8 I'd like everyone to look .... the chart again.
9 10% .... our sales are in Germany.
10 This graph shows sales .... market sector.

Meetings

5

Making arrangements

A: **Are you free on Friday at 3 pm?** Can you make it on Friday at all?

B: I'm afraid I'm busy all day Friday.

A: What about next Tuesday? **Is 3 pm OK with you?**

B: **I'll just check** … Yes that's fine.

I think I'll be able to make it.

Starting a meeting

A: **I'm sorry I'm late.**

B: Don't worry. We're all here now, so let's start. John, **could you take the minutes?**

C: Sure. No problem.

B: **There are four main items on the agenda.** Anita, can we start with your report? Tell us what's been happening …

Can we skip the next item? I have to be at another meeting in half an hour.

Thoughts and opinions (1)

A: **What do you think about this?**

B: I don't really have an opinion!

A: **Do you have any comments?**

B: I think it's an excellent idea.

A: **What's your opinion?**

B: I'm not very happy about it.

I'd like to hear everyone's views on our new advertising campaign.

Thoughts and opinions (2)

A: **I'd like to make a point.**

B: Sure.

A: **I'm very concerned about the current plans.** We need to bring in someone from outside to look at them before we agree to go ahead.

B: **I agree with you,** but we are already behind schedule. Do you have anyone in mind?

If anyone doesn't agree with the proposals, please say so now.

Moving things on

A: **So does anyone have anything else to say?**

B: I suggest we vote on it now.

C: **I suggest we leave it till the next meeting.**

D: **I'm in favour of that.**

B: Well I'm not. I'm against any delay. We need to make a decision today.

We need more time to consider this. We can't rush things.

Coming to a close

A: Are there any more points? **Have we covered everything?**

B: **I have nothing to add.**

C: Neither have I.

D: Just one thing. I'd like to remind everyone that the next meeting will be on Monday afternoon.

A: Thanks, I'd forgotten that. So, if everyone agrees, **I'd like to leave it there.**

The next meeting

A: **We need to arrange the date of the next meeting.**

B: What about Monday, December 9?

A: December the ninth? I'll check my calendar.

C: **Yes, that would be fine.** There's nothing in my diary for that day.

D: **That suits me.**

A: **I can make it** as long as it is **in the morning**, say at 9 o'clock.

I can't make the morning, but 2 o'clock in the afternoon would be good.

Review 5

A Key verbs. Complete the sentences.

*leave consider make suggest delay
remind skip rush*

1 Are there any other issues we need to .... ?
2 Let's .... item 3 on the agenda till the next meeting.
3 Can we .... the next point? I need to do some more research.
4 Can everyone .... June 14?
5 We need more time. We mustn't ..... .
6 I .... that we should not discuss this until everyone has read the report.
7 I need to .... everyone that next week's meeting is cancelled.
8 We cannot .... the decision any longer.

B Key prepositions. Complete the sentences.

in on behind about of with at for

1 We are seriously .... schedule on the project.
2 What kind of timescale are we looking .... ?
3 I'm mainly concerned .... possible delays.
4 I'm not in favour .... starting immediately.
5 We need to set a date .... the next meeting.
6 We need to agree .... a strategy.
7 I suggest that we bring .... an outside expert.
8 Is a morning meeting OK .... you?

C Key prepositions. Complete the sentences.

against   on (3)   in (2)   with   at

1 There are too many items .... the agenda.
2 I think we need to take a vote .... it.
3 I don't have anything .... your suggestions.
4 I have to be at another meeting .... twenty minutes.
5 I don't agree .... that idea.
6 I'd like to move .... to the next point.
7 What kind of changes did you have .... mind?
8 Let's agree to meet again next week .... 3 o'clock.

Expressions
of
time

6

How long have you been here?

Asking about time from a point in the past until now

- Since last Tuesday.

- I arrived the day before yesterday.

- I arrived late last night.

- I've been here (for) nearly three months.

- Ages!

Have you been waiting long?

When did you arrive?

Asking about a point of time in the past

- Three weeks ago.

- Last Tuesday.

- Early this morning.

- My flight got in at 9 o'clock last night.

- I've only just arrived.

My flight has just landed. I'll be with you in ten minutes.

How long are you here for?

Asking about time from now to a point in the future

- Just a week.

- Until the end of the week.

- Until next Tuesday.

- For a couple of days.

- For three and a half months.

You're just here for two days, aren't you?

When are you leaving?

Asking about a point of time in the future

- At four fifteen/a quarter past four.

- Just after/before half past two.

- In two hours'/two weeks' time.

- The day after tomorrow.

- On Monday next week.

- I'm afraid I have to leave soon/straight away.

- I have to go at 4.15.

I'm hoping to catch the 5 o'clock train.

When will the report be ready?

Asking about a point of time in the future

- It should be ready by 4 o'clock.

- By this time next week.

- Sometime this afternoon.

- At the end of the week.

- It probably won't be ready until the beginning of next year.

- It's almost finished.

- Your guess is as good as mine.

I hope to
have finished
by the end of
next week.

Some US/UK differences

- I'll see you **on April third.** (the third of April)

- The office is open **Monday through Friday.** (Monday to Friday)

- What's happening **on the weekend**? (at the weekend)

- Call me at **ten after**/past four. (ten past four)

- **Did you finish** already? (Have you already finished?)

US English	(UK English)

5/4/2003 – Is that the fourth of May or the fifth of April?

5/4/2003	=	fourth of May (US)
	=	fifth of April (UK)

Review 6

Complete the sentences.

in (2)   *at*   *until*   *by*   *to*   *on*   *for*   (−)   *of*

1 We need the document .... 5 pm at the latest.
2 I'm leaving .... the end of the week.
3 My flight leaves .... two hours' time.
4 Will you be in the office .... Tuesday afternoon?
5 I'll be here .... another three hours.
6 I'll phone you .... the morning.
7 I won't be back .... next Monday.
8 See you .... next week.
9 They are arriving at a quarter .... one.
10 Everything will be ready by the beginning .... next year.

Some
useful
sayings

Body language

- Can you **keep an eye on** things while I'm away?

  Can you look after things …

- In our organisation **the right hand never knows what the left is doing.**

  One part of the organisation doesn't know what another part is doing.

- David Sandon doesn't **head up** the company any more. He left two months ago.

  David Sandon is not in charge of the company any more …

- I really **put my foot in it** when I mentioned the retirement party. It was supposed to be a surprise.

  I made a bad mistake …

Time

Things are so busy at work that **we've all
been working round the clock[1]**. Everyone is
working overtime. **It's only a question of
time[2]** before people become so tired that
they will have **to take time off work[3]**. It's
time we all slowed down.

1 working very long hours
2 it will definitely happen
3 not be able to come to work, perhaps because of illness

Time is running out!

Money

Our marketing department has been spending money like water[1] and as a result the company is now **in the red**[2]. They seem to think they have a **licence to print money**[3], but now we're all learning a hard lesson. **Money doesn't grow on trees**[4], you know.

1 spending too much money
2 losing money
3 the right to spend as much as they like
4 money has to be earned

Business
Phrases
Index

Write these sentences in your own language

1 A business trip

DIRECTIONS TO THE OFFICE

How do I get to your office?

_____

I'll send you a map.

_____

Call me if you have any problems.

_____

ARRANGING TO MEET A VISITOR

How are you planning to come tomorrow?

_____

That's a good idea.

_____

Let me know what time your train arrives.

_____

What time does your flight arrive?

_____

I'll wait for you in Arrivals.

Call me when you're in the Baggage Hall.

Can I pick you up from the hotel?

I can make my own way.

If I get lost, I'll phone you!

SECURITY AND RECEPTION

Do I need a security pass to get in?

Ask for me when you arrive at the security gate.

I'll meet you at the reception desk.

I'm here to see Mr Stewart.

FINDING THE OFFICE

Take the lift to the fifth floor.

Turn left out of the lift.

The marketing department is on the next floor up.

INTRODUCTIONS

Have you met our human resources manager?

Joanna has been with us for five years.

She's in charge of personnel matters.

Let me introduce my colleague.

Good to meet you.

How are you settling in?

MAKING CONVERSATION

I'm responsible for staff development.

I report to her.

Give her my regards when you next see her.

How long are you going to be in Helsinki?

I'd like to stay longer.

Is this your first visit?

WELCOMING

I'd like to welcome you to Inertia Manufacturing.

Thank you all for coming.

You can leave your belongings here.

SAYING THANK YOU
Many thanks for your hospitality.

To show our appreciation, we'd like to present you with a small memento.

That's very kind of you.

PROBLEMS
I'm sorry, I don't remember your name.

Now I remember.

Sorry I missed you earlier.

I'm afraid the conference room is reserved.

I'll just go and check.

Excuse me, I'm not feeling very well.

2 Telephoning

MAKING A PHONE CALL
Hello, is that John?

It's about my trip to Warsaw next week.

I was just about to ring you.

ASKING IF SOMEONE IS AVAILABLE
I'll get her for you.

I'm afraid she isn't at her desk.

She's on another line.

She'll be back in the office next week.

TRANSFERRING A CALLER
Would you like to speak to his assistant?

Just a moment, I'll put you through.

Hold on please, I'll transfer you.

LEAVING MESSAGES
I'm afraid I can't make the meeting.

Could you call me back when you get this message?

This is a message for Elinor Olvera.

It's John from Compass Securities returning your call.

Can you ring me when you get this?

This is just to let you know …

If this is a problem, could you give me a call on … ?

I thought it might be useful.

Could you let me know when it arrives?

Just to say that I got your message.

CALLING BACK
Thanks for calling earlier.

I picked up your message.

If I can get hold of her, I'll ring you back later this afternoon.

PHONE PROBLEMS

Is this a good time to talk?

You're breaking up.

Reception is very bad here.

Your switchboard was closed.

It's a very bad line.

We might get cut off.

3 E-mail and the Internet

E-MAIL ADDRESSES

What's your e-mail address?

I'll be away next week but my mail will be forwarded.

SHORT E-MAIL MESSAGES

Thanks for the message.

What about Tuesday morning?

Let me know if that suits you.

Just a quick message.

I'm planning to send you the report as an attachment.

If I don't hear from you, I'll take it that this is OK.

This is to let you know that …

Thanks for sending me the details.

If you need to get me on my mobile, the number is …

SURFING THE NET
I couldn't download the information I needed.

There was something wrong with my printer.

INSTRUCTIONS
Click on the orange icon.

Press the arrow key.

Hold down the 'Alt' key.

Don't forget to back up your work.

WHERE IS IT?
It's in the top left hand corner of the screen.

It's just above the 'Edit' button.

It's right in the middle of the screen.

COMPUTER PROBLEMS
Our server is down at the moment.

My computer screen keeps freezing.

My computer has crashed.

I keep getting an error message.

What version of the software are you using?

You need to load a later version.

4 Presenting

BEGINNINGS
I'd like to tell you something about what we do here.

First of all, I'll give you an overview of the company.

Please feel free to ask questions.

GRAPHS
Have a look at this graph.

The year is shown on the horizontal axis.

The overall trend is upwards.

CHARTS
This chart compares sales by geographical area.

Compare the chart with the one I showed you earlier.

What percentage of sales goes to Argentina?

TABLES
Here are some other statistics.

As you can see from the table …

The figures demonstrate …

MOVING ON
Let's move on to the next slide.

I'd like to come back to that later.

Could you turn to page 9?

ASKING QUESTIONS
Can I ask a question?

Go ahead.

I'd like to go back to something you said earlier.

CLARIFICATION
Can you explain what 'biztecno' means?

Is it something to do with technology?

_____

What does BMES stand for?

_____

ENDINGS
That's all I wanted to say for now.

_____

Is there anything else you would like to cover?

_____

I hope that this session has been informative.

_____

PROBLEMS
I'm sorry, but I can't see the screen very well.

_____

If you give me your address, I'll send it to you.

_____

First we need to check if it is plugged in.

_____

5 Meetings

MAKING ARRANGEMENTS
Are you free on Friday at 3 pm?

Is 3 pm OK with you?

I'll just check ...

STARTING A MEETING
I'm sorry I'm late.

Could you take the minutes?

There are four main topics on the agenda.

THOUGHTS AND OPINIONS

What do you think about this?

_____

Do you have any comments?

_____

What's your opinion?

_____

I'd like to make a point.

_____

I'm very concerned about the current plans.

_____

I agree with you.

_____

MOVING THINGS ON

So does anyone have anything else to say?

_____

I suggest we leave it till the next meeting.

_____

I'm in favour of that.

COMING TO A CLOSE
Have we covered everything?

I have nothing to add.

I'd like to leave it there.

THE NEXT MEETING
We need to arrange the date of the next meeting.

Yes, that would be fine.

That suits me.

I can make it in the morning.

6 Expressions of time

How long have you been here?

_____

When did you arrive?

_____

How long are you here for?

_____

When are you leaving?

_____

When will the report be ready?

_____

Answers

Review 1
1 for   2 of   3 to   4 to   5 with   6 to   7 in   8 of

Review 2
A 1 cut   2 catch   3 get   4 hold   5 leave   6 dial
   7 put   8 ring   9 say   10 talk
B 1j   2i   3d   4a   5e   6c   7h   8f   9g   10b

C 1 with 2 off 3 for 4 up 5 on 6 on 7 off
  8 through

Review 3

A 1 date 2 attachment 3 format 4 scan 5 menu
  6 wrong 7 corner 8 key
B Suggested order: d, c, f, a, b, e
C 1 at 2 on 3 in 4 under 5 up 6 at 7 out
  8 to 9 with 10 from

Review 4

1 about 2 of 3 on 4 in 5 from 6 for 7 for 8 at
9 of 10 by

Review 5

A 1 consider 2 leave 3 skip 4 make 5 rush
  6 suggest 7 remind 8 delay
B 1 behind 2 at 3 about 4 of 5 for 6 on 7 in
  8 with
C 1 on 2 on 3 against 4 in 5 with 6 on 7 in
  8 at

Review 6

1 by 2 at 3 in 4 on 5 for 6 in 7 until 8 –
9 to 10 of